How To Get a Job in Congress

(without winning an election)

By Christopher Porter
Founder and CEO, www.YourCongress.com

Blutarsky Media

Layout, design, and illustrations by
William Porch Design

Library of Congress Card Number:
00-191101
ISBN: 0970154607

Blutarsky Media
P.O. Box 1661
Arlington, VA 22210

Printed in the USA

Table of Contents

HOW TO GET A JOB IN CONGRESS

(WITHOUT WINNING AN ELECTION)

Preface

Maybe it was watching the Iran-Contra hearings on TV in 1986. Maybe it was seeing my college roommate's freshly laminated ID identifying him as a bonafide Congressional intern. Maybe it was my own internship, two full days doing schlep work jammed in between a full course load at American University in Washington.

Whatever it was that attracted me to Capitol Hill, 15 years and three Members of Congress later, I was an official Capitol Hill veteran. I had held virtually every position you could hold in a Congressional office. I even had a few bills and projects that I could say I had a hand in making happen.

This book will tell you what it's like to work on Congressional staff and what it takes to get a job on Capitol Hill. Working on Capitol Hill is far from glamorous — the pay is bad, the hours are hellacious, and Members of Congress can be, by and large, crazy. But for some reason — probably the same reason that kept me hanging my hat in Congress for so long — people clamor for positions on the Hill.

How badly do people want to work on the Hill? Consider this: when I was Chief of Staff for a Member of Congress (a Representative in the U.S. House), I placed a classified ad for a front desk position — someone who answers the phone and takes visitors on tours for about $20,000 a year. The advertised position is as low on the totem pole as you can get, real front line work. Within one day I received over 200 resumes, including two from people with PhDs.

The competition for Hill jobs is fierce, and to compete you need all the help you can get. There is no experience in the world like working in Congress and no more unique challenge than getting a job there. The thing that will separate this book from others, in addition to its revealing inside information, is that it will help you create an individualized plan to get a job on Capitol Hill. It will also give you the skinny on Capitol Hill's working environment, inside tips on interviewing, and a candid look at other Congress-related jobs in Washington.

Currently, there are only a few thousand people in the world who see the Capitol on the nightly news and can say, "Look, it's my office." Every day, these people work in a place where everyone's job is to represent their respective piece of America. These same folks also stand where funny and often embarrassing episodes unfold, most of which are shielded from view. Washington is filled with great stories, some that can never, and should never, be told. With this book and a little hard work, you'll be on the inside in no time and collecting your own stories that can — and can't — be told.

Only the business of politics has the confluence of people, ideas, and competition. And there's no place like Capitol Hill to learn this business, live this life, and get paid for it.

After you've been gainfully employed on the Hill for a couple weeks and we run into each other, I'll buy you a beer at the Tune Inn. We'll swap stories.

Introduction: I Should Have Known Then

When I was just an eighth grade student wearing the required blue pants, blue shirt, and blue tie of Saint Louis Elementary in Cleveland, Ohio, my friend Richard asked me to play Ronald Reagan in our upcoming school debate. Since my Dad was keen on the former California governor, I yielded to Richard's urgings and agreed to play Reagan.

After my initial reluctance to being in the debate ebbed, my competitive juices kicked in. I spent hours at the library compiling the position of Presidential candidate Ronald Reagan. I also conducted research on my opposition, hoping to exploit their weaknesses, and developed a strategy based to appeal to the 99% Catholic and heavily Nun-influenced crowd. Late into the night, I practiced in my family's bare basement, the sound of my shaky voice echoing off the walls.

Even though I slept little the night before the debate, my anxieties vanished with the opening statements. I knew instantly that I had prepared more than my opponents. I had a succinct response to almost every question, and neither of my opponents had much to offer. I remember talking about the "misery index," the hostages in Iran, and hitting all the points that I wanted to in my closing statement. Later that afternoon, with the debate long over, all eligible students trudged to the makeshift polling station in the St. Louis Social Hall and cast their ballots.

The next day, following our en masse Hail Mary, Sister Cabrini announced the results of the Mock Election over the school's public address system. Reagan trounced the incumbent President Carter and John Anderson, reflecting his strength with Catholics and Democrats that year. Richard assured me the Reagan victory was sealed by my performance in the debate. I had carried the swing sixth grade by a two-to-one margin. I was ecstatic.

For the very first time, I had tasted politics' sweetest fruit: the connection between personal acts and common purpose. Political work — whether it's on a campaign or in a Congressional office — is all about being part of something much larger than you.

Waiting for the results of any election, mock or otherwise, is a humbling experience. When the polls have closed, and you have a vested interest in the outcome, you realize that The People have spoken, and the only thing that keeps you from knowing what they have said is our feeble process for listening to them. It's what everyone talks about: the Power of the People.

Little did I know that the school debate would get me hooked on working in politics. It taught me two fundamental truths:

1. Words and deeds, in a competitive atmosphere, have tangible results.
2. Working in politics is a hell of a lot of fun.

I.
A Quick Look at Living in Washington

If I think about it a little longer (say, longer than I did in the preface of this book), I knew that I wanted to get a full-time job on Capitol Hill from my first day as an intern for my hometown Representative, Congresswoman Mary Rose Oakar. I was seduced by the aura of the office: the high-minded discussions, the unique people I met, the official buildings and trappings of elected office. Over time, my attraction blossomed into a full-scale love affair. The more I learned, the more my professional star continued to rise, the more I enjoyed being in Congress. In total, I ended up collecting a check for ten years on Capitol Hill.

LIFE IN THE DISTRICT OF COLUMBIA

Before we dive into life on Capitol Hill, let's start with what it's like to live and work in Washington, D.C. Unless a renegade military junta ousts the current government and moves the

Congress to Cleveland or some other city, you're stuck working and living in Washington. In 1984, during my search for a college to attend, I repeatedly read about what a great city Washington was, but I dismissed the rave reviews as marketing frou-frou. Forgive me if I was a little cynical, but I had also read about what a great city Gary, Indiana, was, too. (No offense to you Gary natives, but please, please install giant fans or something around those pungent steel mills near I-80.)

I ended up attending American University in Washington for the same reasons most people choose their college: they let me in and gave me the best deal. Today, 15 years after first setting foot in D.C., I can assure you that Washington is, indeed, a great city in which to live — regardless of whether or not you work on Capitol Hill. The climate is pleasant, although searing heat in July and August offsets short winters. There are beaches within a three-hour drive, mountains within an hour drive, a lively nightlife scene, and more culture than you could ever take in. It's a beautiful city, unlike any other in our country. In terms of architecture, Washington has a strong European flavor but also remains distinctly American.

The main downside to Washington is the cost of living. According to the American Chamber of Commerce, Washington is the fourth most expensive city in the United States (behind Manhattan, San Francisco, and Long Island). In 1985, on my first night in Washington, I remember getting a rude awakening with regard to D.C. prices in a local bar. I ordered a beer, thinking that it would cost the same $1 like back in Ohio, maybe $1.50. The bartender asked for $3. At home, I could get a pitcher of beer for $3. So be prepared.

Rent is expensive. According to the Department of Off-Campus Housing at George Washington University in Washington, a two bedroom apartment averages between $900 and $1300 a month, and a one bedroom goes for $750-$1000. Groceries are inexplicably expensive, being second only to Hawaii (which has to fly in their food). Many people live in close by Virginia or Maryland to help save money, although some of the suburban neighborhoods are more expensive than living in D.C. itself. The best way to save money is to live in a group house, but the trade-off is that you have to deal with all the hassles of group-home living.

Why is D.C. so damn expensive? Washington is a company town, and the company is the federal government. My theory is that because the government is an economic bedrock, all sellers know that there will always be income in the area. Consequently, prices reflect the permanence and presence of money.

Getting around D.C. is easy — with two exceptions: a.) you're in a car, and b.) it's rush hour. Gridlock is not just limited to Congress. D.C. was recently rated as having the second most traffic congestion in the nation. However, public transportation is excellent. Cabs are plentiful and cheap, and the subway system (Metro) is clean, efficient, and works well with an extensive bus system.

Let me add one more thing about D.C. that you may be interested in. Washington is a great place to live at any age, but particularly when you are young. I have been all across America, and there is no other city in our country that has such a concentration of young, smart, motivated individuals. There are so many goal-oriented, fresh-faced college grads in D.C. that it makes people like me (who was prone to cutting class on a whim to play basketball) a little sick to my stomach. But I shouldn't complain, particularly when you also consider matters of the heart. Amid the hub-bub of working in D.C., many young people have met the love of their life in the shadow of the Nation's Capitol. I'm one of them.

II. What Jobs Are Available on Capitol Hill

It may have a few drawbacks, but Washington has one thing that no other city has: the U.S. Congress. And that's why you're reading this book. Let's get to it and take a look at the jobs that are available in the offices of Representatives and Senators.

Within each Congressional Member's office, there are two different job tracks: legislative and administrative. For people trying to secure their job on Capitol Hill, these are the jobs within each track:

LEGISLATIVE TRACK

- ❑ Legislative Assistant
- ❑ Legislative Correspondent
- ❑ Press Secretary

On the Legislative Track, there is also the job of Legislative Director (LD) who oversees the legislative staff. However, no Chief of Staff in their right mind is going to hire an LD who has no Hill experience, so forgettaboutit. We'll touch on the role of the LD later so you know about all the jobs in an office, but we won't treat it like a position that you're going to pursue.

ADMINISTRATIVE TRACK

- ❑ Staff Assistant
- ❑ Scheduler/Executive Assistant
- ❑ Systems Administrator
- ❑ Office Manager

The highest job on the Administrative Track is the Chief of Staff. Be aware that on Capitol Hill, the titles Chief of Staff and AA (or Administrative Assistant) are synonymous. While in the private sector the position of administrative assistant is usually a secretary, on Capitol Hill it is the top of the ladder. To avoid any confusion, most people now use the title Chief of Staff.

The exact role of Chief of Staff varies from office to office, but generally they are the top dog which oversees overall operations of both D.C. and district/home state office(s). A Chief of Staff usually also acts as Supreme Commander of the Legislative track. So, in terms of your job search, I think it's a safe bet to cross this one off your list.

We'll now look at each job on each track in a little more detail.

LEGISLATIVE TRACK POSITIONS

Legislative Assistant

When most people pursue their first job in Congress, their goal is to become a legislative assistant - someone who works with a Representative or Senator on bills and legislation. These are coveted positions. House Members have two or three legislative assistants, or LAs, while Senators tend to have about six or seven. Because this position is the most highly sought after, we will discuss it in great detail.

Each legislative assistant has a number of specific issues, usually between four and eight, assigned to him or her. Each LA is responsible for "covering" these issues. "Covering" an issue means being the Representative or Senator's eyes, ears, and mouth on a particular issue. Specifically, for each assigned issue, a Legislative Assistant is responsible for:

- Being aware of all the bills that are before Congress (usually a few hundred for each issue)
- Reading gobs of mail from constituents and organizations

• Meeting with constituents and lobbyists (often in place of the Congressman/woman or Senator)
• Promoting any bills the Representative or Senator has authored with other Congressional offices, non-profits, trade associations, corporations, or other organizations
• Advising the Congressman/woman or Senator on whether or not to cosponsor (officially support) other Members' legislation
• Advising the Congressman/woman or Senator on how to vote on bills and amendments on the floor
• Communicating the Congressman/woman or Senator's issue positions

Because this is such an extensive list of duties, one of the most important skills every LA needs to develop is prioritization. With all the different issues competing for attention, an LA has to know where to focus his or her energies and what to ignore. In almost all cases, the prioritization skills develop as a LA's relationship grows with the Representative or Senator and his or her superiors in the office.

A WORD ABOUT ISSUES

When I first started working on the Hill, I was surprised at the sheer number of issues that confronted Members of Congress.

In a short amount of time, I discovered that there were universes which revolved around issues that I had never even heard of. All individual LAs are responsible for covering a wide range of subject matter for a Representative or Senator, and quite often are responsible for issues that they initially know absolutely nothing about.

Look at the chart on the next page that lists the major issues a Member of Congress and their staff confront every day on Capitol Hill. The entire table of issues is divided up among a legislative staff so, in theory, the Congresswoman/man or Senator has a "specialist" in every issue.

Keep in mind that each issue has a number of sub-issues. For example, education as an issue consists of early childhood education, K-12 education, college education, and lifelong learning (also called vocational education). If you cover education, you likely cover these other four issues as well — and each has its own supporters and opponents within Congress, the public sector, and the private sector.

Pretty extensive list, eh? Take a few minutes and look through the list. See which issues stand out to you and keep them in the back of your mind. We'll refer to this chart later.

Many offices give every staffer, regardless of their position in

Abortion/Choice
Agriculture
Appropriations Projects
Arts
Banking and Financial Services
Budget
Business
(including small business)
Campaign Finance Reform
Childcare
Crime
Defense
(National Security)
Disabilities
Education
Energy
Environment or Natural
Resources
Gun Control/2nd Amendment
Rights
Health Care
(including Medicare and
Medicaid)
Housing
Human and Civil Rights
Immigration
International Relations
(including Israel)
Judiciary
Labor
Native Americans
Postal Issues
Science and Technology
Social Security and
Retirement
Space
Taxes
Telecommunications and
Internet Trade
Veterans
Welfare
Women's Issues

Inside Info: REGARDLESS OF WHAT POSITION YOU MAY INTERVIEW FOR, ASK IF YOU CAN BE GIVEN AN ISSUE OR TWO TO COVER. MANY OFFICES DO THIS TO HELP DEVELOP INTERNAL OFFICE SKILLS, AND IT SHOWS INITIATIVE.

the office, an issue or two to cover for the Representative or Senator. Issues that don't have great exposure, and consequently have low political risk, are called "starter issues." When I was hired for my first job as a legislative correspondent, I also covered Merchant Marine and Fisheries issues. Because very few bills on this issue came to the floor, it was a good way for me to get exposure to LA work without getting in too much hot water. (The Merchant Marine and Fisheries Committee has since been abolished, so don't ask for this issue.)

COMMITTEE WORK

There's another important wrinkle to a legislative assistant's role in every Congressional office. The legislative assistant who covers the Member's committee assignment (called the Member's "committee work") has a coveted position. For example, if Congressman Schlomoe Lacey were on the Education and Workforce Committee, the LA who covered education would have a plum position — and would be senior to other legislative assistants.

For this reason, in many offices, the Legislative Director handles the brunt of the committee work.

Why is covering committee work a big deal? Doing committee work carries a much higher profile within a Congressional office because, compared to "regular" legislative assistant positions, you have a much higher chance of actually passing legislation that will become law. The LA who handles committee work also gets to participate in committee deliberations called hearings and markups. In hearings, a Congressional committee invites people to come and testify on the public record with their views of a pending bill or issue. In a markup, the committee actually writes the bill itself, going through it line-by-line in a public setting.

The legislative assistant who covers committee work has a luxury that most staff doesn't have: they will handle bills that the committee is considering, or "moving." Out of the thousands of bills that are referred to any individual committee, approximately less than 50 a year get "moved." On a broad level, this means that LAs doing committee work are involved in bills that have a decent chance of becoming law — so the stakes are higher for Members, lobbyists, and organizations. You get the chance to be "in play" when you're in committee.

Inside Info: IN YOUR SEARCH TO GET A JOB ON CAPITOL HILL, IF YOU HAVE THE FORTUNE OF CHOOSING BETWEEN TWO LA JOBS – ONE WITH COMMITTEE WORK AND ONE WITHOUT – TAKE THE ONE THAT INCLUDES COMMITTEE WORK. IT WILL DEFINITELY GIVE YOU GREAT EXPERIENCE FOR YOUR RESUME, AND YOU WILL LIKELY ENJOY IT MORE, TOO.

During the days leading up to a markup, and during the markup itself, an individual LA can work with the committee staff to incorporate their boss' ideas into the pending bill. It is at this point when a good legislative assistant earns his or her pay because committee staffers are usually very reluctant to change a bill once it has been written. During the markup process, persistence and a keen sense for the art of the possible make the difference between securing the section, paragraph, or even single word that is your Member's own idea — and thus getting something done and getting good press — or leaving empty-handed.

On a personal level, the committee work LA has more interaction with the Representative or Senator and can often develop a much closer relationship with him or her than is possible for other staff members. There are other benefits as well. Usually the person who handles committee work gets assigned fewer issues and can gain expertise in a particular subject matter — expertise that can lead to a lucrative job as a lobbyist or an association professional.

Legislative Correspondent

The legislative correspondent, or LC, is the person who is responsible for the one thing that every Capitol Hill office dreads: constituent mail. Because dealing with the mail is such a miserable job, being an LC is the perfect proving ground for a young staffer, and an excellent entrance to the legislative track.

A Congressional office receives a huge amount of correspondence from their constituents asking for the Member's position

on one particular issue or another. Every office has a sophisticated constituent mail system to track and process both constituent inquiries and the relevant responses. Further, every office has their own individual policy on how many people in their office actually write the texts (anywhere from 1 to 8) and how the role of the LC operates within their entire system. The LC is responsible for knowing the computer systems, writing in large quantities, printing in even larger quantities, and the associated folding/stuffing duties. Bottom line: the LC is responsible for getting mail out the door.

There are three reasons why the LC position is ideal for someone seeking to get his or her first job on Capitol Hill, regardless of how an individual office structures their mail system. First, working with the mail provides an exposure to the wide breadth of issues that confront Representatives and Senators, as well as an initially shocking introduction to the array of wackos in the United States who write the federal government (this later gives way to amusement). Writing mail also gives you the chance to hone your basic writing skills, something that all current Hill Chiefs of Staff lament as having generally deteriorated over the last ten years. Last, being an LC also gives you the chance to prove yourself, show that you can tackle a difficult, thankless job.

Press Secretary

I include the position of press secretary, or communications director, as being part of the legislative track, but they are more independent than other positions. Dealing with reporters, writing news releases, and having knowledge of the press, radio, television, and internet media game is an art and a skill all its own. Unless you already have experience in these areas, no one is going to consider hiring you. Press is too important to an individual Representative or Senator's political health to be left to an utter novice.

If you do, however, have some experience — a basic understanding of the print, TV, or radio media game and even a modicum of relevant experience — you probably have a good shot at getting a press job. Good press secretaries are in chronic short supply on the Hill, and even with very little experience they command higher salaries than most legislative assistants.

Legislative Director

The legislative director (LD) is the highest position on the legislative track, and one of the three most important jobs in a Representative or Senator's office (Chief of Staff, Press Secretary, and LD). The LD keeps track of the Member's overall legislative profile

— often with an eye toward the upcoming re-election campaign — and also supervises the other legislative staff Members.

ADMINISTRATIVE TRACK POSITIONS

RECEPTIONIST/STAFF ASSISTANT

The receptionist or staff assistant is the person on the Congressional office's front line. These stalwarts answer phones, greet visitors, arrange tours of Washington monuments for constituents, and do general office work. The receptionist is usually the lowest person on the office totem pole, and they know it. The good thing about taking a staff assistant job is that there's no place to go but up, and Congressional offices like to promote from within. Like the legislative correspondent job, it's a chance to prove you can do a good job in fairly trying circumstances.

SCHEDULER (ALSO CALLED EXECUTIVE ASSISTANT)

The scheduler/executive assistant is the least known job, but one of the most powerful, in any Capitol Hill office. The scheduler/executive assistant's importance comes from being one of the few people who decide what a Representative or Senator does with their time. You see, all Representatives or Senators have far more requests for appearances than they have available time, and the scheduler has the authority to influence who gets in and who does not. All the requests — whether they're from constituents, the media, other Members of Congress, or even their own staff — are funneled through the scheduler. It's a powerful job.

The scheduler/executive assistant also tends to handle many areas of the Member's personal life, so they tend to know a lot — too much, probably — about what these people are really like. After tending to their Congressional responsibilities, campaign responsibilities, and family needs, a Member of Congress has very little time left over for mundane errands. The scheduler often deals with many of these problems. If you can cheerfully buy underwear, balance someone else's family checkbook, or bail out other people's jailed relatives, then the executive assistant/scheduler job is for you.

Office Manager

In many offices, the role of the office manager is often folded into one or more of the other administrative positions. His or her job is to order office supplies, use financial software to keep track of office billings (vouchers), call the service man when the copier is on the fritz, and generally serve as a point of contact for office administrative procedures.

Systems Administrator

The systems administrator is a role that is growing in importance in Congressional offices. A systems administrator works with the numerous computer vendors and information system offices within the House, Senate, and private sector to make certain that all the computer hardware and software applications are functioning within a Congressional office. All Congressional operations (excepting two or three holdouts) have a computer network with eight or nine workstations in the D.C. office, usually connected via a frame relay to an additional six to ten computers in their district office or offices. The systems administrator makes sure that each office is maximizing its individual system. He or she will also spend time answering nettlesome questions from office mates about printers, email, or any other electronic thing that goes haywire. Increasingly, the systems administrator is also the webmaster for the Member's web page.

Chief of Staff/AA

The Chief of Staff holds a position that will be crucial to your job search for the obvious reason that he or she makes the hiring decisions. Sometimes they have the authority to hire someone without the Representative or Senator's approval, other times they provide recommendations and leave the decision to the Member. In either case, you can be certain that the Chief of Staff is the most important person in the hiring process.

ADMINISTRATIVE TRACK VS. LEGISLATIVE TRACK

Now that you know about the two tracks for jobs on Capitol Hill, you need to keep an additional item in mind. All entry-level jobs, on either the administrative or legislative track, can serve as a means of proving one's self to an individual office — demonstrating the ability to work in a Congressional work environment. However, if you spend a considerable amount of time (say, more than two years) on the administrative track, it's going to be much harder for you to switch to the legislative track. You will have proved your worth, but you

Inside Info: TO AVOID GETTING STUCK ON THE ADMINISTRATIVE TRACK, MAKE CERTAIN THAT YOU MAKE IT CLEAR TO YOUR SUPERIORS FROM THE GET-GO THAT ALTHOUGH YOU ARE DELIGHTED AND HAPPY WITH THE POSITION YOU HAVE ACCEPTED, YOU HOPE THAT YOU WILL HAVE THE CHANCE TO BE CONSIDERED FOR THE NEXT AVAILABLE LEGISLATIVE POSITION. WHEN THE LEGISLATIVE POSITION THAT YOU WANT OPENS, FIRMLY REMIND YOUR SUPERIORS (WHO WILL PROBABLY HAVE FORGOTTEN) OF YOUR INTEREST AND GO FOR IT.

will have likely acquired highly valuable skills that are hard to replace (for example, dealing with a Member of Congress' schedule). Very few offices will want to give up these skills. It is not impossible to go from one track to the other, but it's better to do a short stint in an administrative position and then move to the legislative track within a year or two, if that's where you ultimately want to be.

You can almost always go from the legislative to the administrative track with little difficulty. However, be prepared to explain why you want to switch because legislative track positions are more highly sought after than administrative jobs.

III.
Eight Things You Need to Know

Now you've got it all figured out. You know what position you want and you have a better understanding of what the various jobs are all about. In fact, my friend, the real work has just begun. There's more you need to consider before you load up the truck and move to Washington, D.C. You need to get familiar with the unique working environment of the place we call Congress. Dealing with Members of Congress and Congressional responsibilities may be fascinating work, but it's not something to just dive into willy-nilly. You can thank me later.

1. MEMBERS OF CONGRESS TEND TO BE INSANE.

I believe most successful people tend to be a little off the deep end, and Members of Congress are no different. Don't get me wrong. I have worked for two great Congresswomen and one great Congressman on Capitol Hill, people that I truly respect and for whom I have tremendous affection. That said, the plain fact is that the job of being a Member of Congress tends to make people a little, well, crazy.

For a moment, put yourself in their shoes. Many people decide to run for Congress with little or no knowledge of the demands it places on their personal lives. It takes an extraordinary amount of time and effort to get elected, even when a candidate doesn't face serious opposition. Every candidate has to spend an enormous amount of time raising money, doing appearances, and generally working like a dog to be elected. Whenever you seek something that someone else wants — and a baffling amount of people want to be a Representative or Senator — you have to be prepared to fight for it.

The immediate family of most successful candidates believe that things will "get better" after the election, that their father or mother will be able to actually spend time with them. Wrong. In reality, things only get more hectic. Members of Congress tend to be "scheduled" for most of their life. When Congress is in session, they're working from 7AM to 7PM. When Congress isn't in session, they're doing appearances and meetings in their district to maintain "visibility." For practical reasons, much of their life is turned over to their staff. This is a very difficult situation for any family, particularly one with children. And from the second they take office, at least in the House with its two-year terms, it's a race for re-election. It's a train that is very difficult to stop, even if they did want to get off. In almost all cases, these pressures make an individual Representative or Senator a little nutty.

It varies from Member-to-Member, but on a daily basis a staffer has to be prepared to deal with the possibility of fits of dementia. Every now and then you will hear your boss make outlandish statements, and you can count on being in the vicinity of a blown stack from time to time. You have to get thick skin and develop a "get it done" mentality or the press of events could weigh you down.

2. D, R, OR I? YOU HAVE TO CHOOSE SIDES

I still believe what I always have: there are good Members of Congress and bad Members of Congress in both political parties. Neither the Republican Party nor the Democratic Party has cornered the market on sainthood or buffoonery.

What I didn't realize until I got to Capitol Hill, even after earning a degree in political science, is the stratification of Congress between the party in power, the Majority, and the party not in power, the Minority — and what this means to an individual staffer. (Until at least January of 2001, the Republicans have the Majority in both the House and the Senate.) This division has important career implications that you should fully consider before pursuing a position on Capitol Hill.

Let me step back a moment to my young, heady days. When I got out of college, I knew I wanted to work on Capitol Hill. My lack of a solid political stripe led me to interview with both Republicans and Democrats. While things worked out just fine for me, I wouldn't recommend that you do this. Bear with me, as this one takes a bit of an explanation.

Before I worked on the Hill, I assumed that there were a plethora of non-partisan jobs that made Congress tick — people not affiliated with any party that served both Democrats and Republicans equally. In reality, there are a scant few of these types of jobs. The Majority controls most non-partisan jobs — not all, but most. Nearly everyone on Capitol Hill works for someone who is identified with one party or the other.

The effect of the Majority-Minority split is most profound on legislative staff. Professional contacts — which become the lifeblood of a legislative staffer's ability to be effective — are almost exclusively within one party. On its surface, this doesn't seem to be a big deal, but it is. Read on.

"You've got to build insiders on these committees," my first boss would constantly yell at me. The ability of a legislative assistant to get anything done on Capitol Hill depends on his or her relationships with other staffs, particularly committee staff members. Each committee has two staffs: a majority staff and a minority staff. (In the current Congress, the minority staff serves the Democrats and the majority staff serves the Republicans. Independents must choose one party with which to affiliate.) As a result, the bulk of experience a legislative assistant gains is with Members and staff of their own party. You can call the staff of the other party, and this is often done when two individual Members are trying to accomplish something together. But the committee staff of the other party, who make key decisions about what their side (their Chairman) will and won't support, and ultimately what can and can't be placed in bills, have no desire to help you because they are busy handling requests from

Members of their own party. It's a weeding out function. Everyone is so busy that each side takes care of its own people.

As a staff member, once your contacts are cultivated, they are all on one side of the aisle or the other. You have little or no value to your boss when your professional contacts are with people that don't want to help you.

Let me give you an example of what I mean.

In 1999, Mike Forbes, a Congressman from New York, switched political parties. He was a Republican and became a Democrat. Immediately after his

DON'T FRET IF YOU DON'T KNOW WHETHER YOU'RE A DEMOCRAT, REPUBLICAN, LIBERTARIAN, OR COMMUNIST. I WAS IN YOUR SHOES ONCE, TOO. I LEFT COLLEGE A VERY POLITICALLY CONFUSED LAD. SO WHEN I WAS FACED WITH CHOOSING A POLITICAL PARTY, I TESTED THE WATERS. I INTERNED TWO DAYS A WEEK IN A DEMOCRATIC OFFICE, AND FOUND THAT THE WATER WAS JUST FINE. WHILE I DIDN'T AGREE WITH EVERYTHING, I FELT COMFORTABLE WITH THEIR OVERALL PRINCIPLES. (ACTUALLY, I FOUND MY ANSWER IN THE EXTREMES. I COULD HANDLE OUT-OF-TOUCH LEFT-WINGERS MUCH EASIER THAN RACIST RIGHT-WINGERS.) SO IF YOU FACE THIS DILEMMA, TEST THE WATERS AND GO WHERE THINGS FEEL RIGHT. THERE ARE LIBERAL TO CONSERVATIVE RANGES IN BOTH MAJOR POLITICAL PARTIES, AND A FEW ALTERNATIVE POLITICAL PARTIES. IF YOU FIND YOURSELF IN THE WRONG SITUATION, KEEP MOVING AROUND UNTIL YOU FIND THE RIGHT ONE.

announcement, his entire staff quit. His staff's action was a result of more than just simple anger at Forbes' party betrayal. In fact, Forbes had, in one move, negated all their jobs. Staying on with Forbes the Democrat would be impossible because the stratification in Congress between the Majority and the Minority would ensure that they did not have the professional contacts to do their jobs. His staff was faced with a choice: completely start over with a new party and build all new professional contacts, or start over with another Republican Congressman/woman and maintain their professional contacts. Their only choice was to find new Republicans to work for — which they did with little problem.

Bottom line: once you're aligned with one party or the other, it's nearly impossible to switch back. So if you're first job is with a Democrat, you're a professional Democrat. If your first job is with a Republican, you're a professional Republican.

3. KA-CHING? TRY KAPUT.

No one gets rich working on Capitol Hill. Congress compensates by giving you unique work experience, not loads of cash.

In 1990, I accepted my first paid job on Capitol Hill as Legislative Correspondent for $16,000 a year. I swallowed a 25%

pay cut to take this position — taking home $1,034 every month, of which $408 went to rent.

Living on $150 a week in Washington is nearly impossible, but somehow I did it. In essence, I gave up short-term money to get my foot in the door of Congress, and it was one of the best moves I ever made. Had I been concerned about reaching a certain salary number, I probably would not have been able to get any job on the Hill. Keep in mind that the current labor shortage that is pushing up entry-level wages in many places in America does not exist on Capitol Hill. There are still plenty of people who are seeking a short supply of jobs.

Each individual Representative or Senator can pay their staff whatever they want, as long as it's not more than the maximum (as of the year 2000 $141,300 a year). Some Members are cheapskates, some are generous, and many are fair.

Like most Chiefs of Staff, I would always collude with my colleagues about pay. I was consistently in step with the averages, so I can give you a guideline of what to expect in terms of money. If I hired you as a new staff-assistant or LC, I would try to pay you as little as possible. There are plenty of people who kill for these jobs, and it's not rocket science, so I would pay you no less than $20K and no more than $25K. For a fresh-faced LA, I'd try to pay you around $25K with no experience and might go up to $30K or so with a little experience. Again, there's an abundant supply of people who want to be LAs, but the work is a little more substantial so it garners a higher salary. I always paid schedulers/executive assistants well because a good one helps the entire organization function well, and it's a tough job. If the scheduler job also includes many of the office manager functions, expect to make no less than $28K and up to $32K to start with no experience. Depending on the responsibilities, a systems administrator will make mid 20's, and an office manager in the high 20's or low 30's. In my experience, the press secretary position has the broadest salary range. Generally expect to make at least $28K, but likely in the low-to-mid $30K's.

I warn you that these figures are only estimates. In general, Senate salaries for the comparable positions are likely to be a little higher, but not necessarily.

There is a non-profit organization called the Congressional Management Foundation (CMF) which exists to "help Congressional offices improve management practices." CMF conducts a number of surveys of all personal offices in the House and Senate, and provides aggregate data for each position in a Representative or Senator's office. They also have extensive House and

Senate staff employment salary data — some of which is available on the web. You can order CMF products, which include salary ranges and breakdown based on experience, from their web page: http://www.c-m-f.org.

4. JOB CONDITIONS ON CAPITOL HILL BLOW

Prior to 1995, all the laws about worker safety and the minimum wage didn't apply to Congress. I'm not kidding, Congress actually exempted itself from all these laws. That changed with the passage of the Shays Act in 1995 and Congress now complies with federal law, although there are special circumstances about how it applies to Congress in some areas.

While Congressional employees now enjoy most of the same worker protections as other workers, employment in Congress can be tough. Congress is an "at will" employer, meaning you serve at the will of the Member. Outside of federal law protections from discrimination, you can be fired for almost any reason at any time.

Second, the conditions are cramped. Most offices on the House side have eight or nine people and all office equipment stuck into approximately 600 or 800 square feet. Most job descriptions include a clause which says that you have "no expectations of personal privacy." Don't try to keep a secret on Capitol Hill.

Inside Info: WORKING FROM 8AM TO 8PM IS STANDARD FOR MOST HILL OFFICES, PARTICULARLY WHEN CONGRESS IS IN SESSION. CONGRESS IS USUALLY IN SESSION ABOUT THREE-FIFTHS OF THE YEAR. WHEN CONGRESS IS NOT IN SESSION, CALLED "DISTRICT WORK PERIODS," OFFICES ARE MUCH MORE RELAXED. THE REPRESENTATIVE OR SENATOR IS OFTEN BACK IN THE HOME STATE, AND HIS OR HER STAFF WORKS A SCHEDULE THAT IS MORE BEARABLE — USUALLY 9AM – 6PM.

Last, for any position that you accept, count on working long hours and enduring many stressful, crazy moments. It's common for Hill staffers to work from 8AM until 8PM or later. Washington is a "workaholic" city and people thrive on staying late. The implication is that the later you work, the more important you are. Many people are surprised when they find out that when Congress is in session, rush hour in D.C. lasts until 7:30PM.

Frankly, one of the reasons I had to leave Capitol Hill is that I never saw my family. I would routinely come home after my son's 8PM bedtime. So be prepared.

One caveat to the less-than-stellar job conditions: while you can't get stock options, Congressional offices do offer a solid benefits package. Everyone gets health insurance through the Federal Employee Health Benefit Program which offers a wide range of plans, and you are responsible for only 25% of your premium each month. All staff have guaranteed access to group life insurance and the Thrift Savings Plan (a beefed up 401K for federal employees). Each office sets own vacation and sick policies.

5. MY BOSS, MYSELF

Imagine an organization where the CEO is in touch with every person in his or her organization every day. Most Congressional offices are like this. On the House side of the Capitol, the distance between a Member and his or her staff is very small — the quarters are cramped and there are only eight or nine people on the entire staff. Because Senate offices are much larger, with about 30 people in an office, the number of people who have interaction with the Senator on a daily basis is much more limited. But in both cases, the main personality driving the organization is close to the people who do the work.

The close and frequent contact between a Representative or Senator and his or her staff has an interesting result, one that personally affects you, the employee. Because Congressional offices are personality-driven organizations in close quarters, a staff often takes on the personality of the Member. If your boss is a jerk, you will likely become a jerk, too. (This makes research on a prospective employer important, which we'll get to in a little bit.) This transformation can be slow, and can be undetected.

On a day-to-day basis, this also means that offices have to deal with the mood of their boss. Unlike a company where the CEO or Executive Director exists in their own universe separate from most of the peons, Congressional offices feel the immediate result of their boss' temperament. Depending on your boss' predisposition to mood swings, it can be a wild, emotional ride.

6. RELATIVE AGONY

Working on Capitol Hill instantly qualifies you as a bottom-rung celebrity. At this level of stardom, you are involved in something that is just different enough to be interesting but not grand enough to invoke awe. As a result, you will encounter a number of hassles endured by celebrities without getting any of the perks.

You will be inundated with requests. Just because you work

on Capitol Hill, every person that you've ever known will expect that you can get him or her to meet the Speaker or get tickets to the exclusive art show at the National Gallery of Art or secure the President's Box at the Kennedy Center. Some of these requests will be doable while others will be absolutely impossible.

Handling personal requests is easy compared to dealing with the need of your relatives to unload on you their frustrations with the federal government. You will start to dread talking about work at home because people will personally blame you for any of the problems in Washington. You will also learn more about your relatives' personal beliefs than you ever wanted to know. You've done just fine this far in your life without knowing that Uncle Joe has strong opinions on this or that ethnic group, but with your new position you're going to learn more than you ever wanted.

7. THINK YOU'RE IMPORTANT? GET ME SOME COFFEE

Let's face it: most people who work on the Hill have a little, maybe just a little, teensy, weensy bit of vanity. I warn you, if think you're going to get into Washington and become some giant stud or studdette, you've got another thing coming. Any good staffer gets ahead by doing one thing: serving their Representative or Senator. And any good staffer knows that this means more than just helping write good legislation or getting press attention. It means doing whatever it takes to keep that Representative or Senator comfortable in their job.

Let me explain what I mean. I remember being in a Committee markup where we had just passed major legislation that we had worked on for literally three years — a bill where billions of dollars and millions of people's lives were at stake. As the markup wound down, and we were about to go meet the press, my boss pulled me aside and said, "I could really use some coffee." Without hesitation, I went and got it. Members of Congress don't care what your title is; they only care whether or not you're handy when an idea pops into their head.

I have a friend who wields a fair amount of power as Chief of Staff to a Representative who chairs one of the four most powerful committees in Congress. Whenever they travel overseas, he has to taste any food that his boss doesn't recognize — not for poison, but just for taste.

So if you're going to Capitol Hill to grow your hat size, let me tell you the truth: it'll shrink in a hurry.

8. TAKE YOUR PICK: GET NAUSEOUS OR RESTORE YOUR FAITH IN DEMOCRACY

Congress, particularly the House, is a very raw institution. The Senate tries to stay above the fray, but it still has moments when it descends into the abyss. When the business of Congress becomes your business, once or twice a year you will witness moments when everything gets stripped away and the real inner beliefs of a Representative or Senator are revealed.

Unfortunately, sometimes these moments are not a pleasant experience. I have vivid memories of Members running away, sometimes literally, from tough votes — acting so selfish that it made me sick to my stomach. I experienced media feeding-frenzies, instigated by half-truths and enabled by lazy reporting, that wrought havoc with lives. Occasionally, it can get ugly.

More often, however, these revealing moments are heartening. I have a list of personal highlights from the floor of Congress. I lived through the gut-wrenching debate over the Persian Gulf War, when Representatives and Senators — with no political certainty to guide them — were forced to speak from their heart. I have seen individual Representatives and Senators, often people that I didn't expect, make speeches on controversial issues so eloquent that they harkened to the days of Patrick Henry.

There are also moments in which you seem to be a part of history. As an intern, I watched Members of Congress start to cry upon hearing the news that the Space Shuttle had exploded. I witnessed, first-hand, as Boris Yeltsin addressed Congress as the first Russian President — only three weeks after he stood on the tank in Moscow and stared down the entire Soviet regime. I saw Nelson Mandela address the U.S. Congress as the President of South Africa, and had the good fortune of being able to see him address his own Parliament in Cape Town, South Africa.

And I've seen Members, without taking a stitch of credit, turn individual lives around. I've seen health care coverage denials turn into successful operations. I've seen elected officials help ordinary people transform tears of grief over a child's unnecessary death into tears of joy. Most importantly, I've seen that when the right people are in the right place at the right time, the American system of government can work the way we want it to work.

There's a little saint and a little snake in all of us, and Congress can feed either one. It's up to you to decide which one.

IV.
The Plan

When I worked on Capitol Hill, the one thing I always did, from my first day as an intern to my last day as Chief of Staff, was help people find jobs. Friends and relatives would call and ask me to help a friend or relative get a job on Capitol Hill. I counseled hundreds of people and was always gratified when someone with whom I worked found employment. After all, I had been there myself.

I've personally sought a job on Capitol Hill, I've helped other people get jobs on Capitol Hill, and I've hired people for jobs on Capitol Hill. I want to use my knowledge of every side to help you get the position you want.

All this experience helped me devise a plan that will get you a job on Capitol Hill. Like anything that's worth doing, it's not easy. If it were easy, someone else would have already done it. It's not a plan for wimps, but I bet you would have stopped reading by now if you weren't tough. So let's go for it.

Before we begin, let's clarify our goal. This plan has three phases with the ultimate goal of getting your foot in the door with a paid position. Once you're in the working environment of Capitol Hill, in any position whatsoever, you are automatically fulfilling two important Congressional career-enhancing functions. First, you are building "Hill Experience" — learning the game and the players — something that bolsters the odds of any future position in Washington that is government-related.

Second, because you are part of the Hill community, you will hear about open positions before anyone else does. As a result, you have an even better chance of securing a position that is the right fit for you. It's just like working within a company and hearing about job openings at the water cooler before they're advertised to the outside world. Once you secure a job on Capitol Hill, any job whatsoever, it is relatively easy to move into a better situation in another office.

STEP 1. CONSIDER FREE LABOR

The first step of the Plan doesn't require anything but your thinking caps, so put down your Number 2 pencils for the time being. We need to discuss something that could be your ticket to fame and fortune in D.C.: free labor. Washington loves people to come and work for free — it's called an internship. My money says that D.C. has more openings for internships than any other city in the world. (Hmmm. Living in a Southern city and working your butt off at a cruddy job for no pay — doesn't this ring a bell?)

I bring this issue up now because, hands down, the best way to get a job in Congress is to do an internship on Capitol Hill. For those of you who were busy watching MTV or downloading porn or generally not paying attention, I repeat:

Hands down, the best way to get a job in Congress is to do an internship on Capitol Hill.

Honestly, every single person I know who did a Congressional internship and wanted a paid position on Capitol Hill succeeded in getting a job on Capitol Hill. (The only exception to this rule I could envision is someone who is a complete moron or social degenerate. Since you bought this book, I'm pretty sure you're neither.)

Earlier, I mentioned the goal of getting on the inside of Congress.

An internship allows you to accrue almost the same career-enhancing benefits as if you were a paid staff assistant, only for no salary. In addition, there's a decent chance that the office which gave you the internship — even though they might have said they don't have any openings — will eventually offer you a paid position. Capitol Hill offices are so busy and pressed for time that they get used to having a dependable extra hand around.

Inside Info: IT'S MUCH EASIER TO GET AN INTERNSHIP IN A CONGRESSIONAL OFFICE DURING THE FALL, WINTER, AND SPRING THAN IT IS DURING THE SUMMER. MOST OFFICES ARE INUNDATED WITH APPLICATIONS FOR SUMMER INTERNSHIP POSITIONS – USUALLY FAR MORE APPLICATIONS THAN AVAILABLE SPACE. WHILE IT'S NOT ALWAYS THE CASE, SUMMER INTERNSHIPS ARE OFTEN USED AS POLITICAL FAVORS FOR THE RELATIVES OF BIG SUPPORTERS. STILL, DON'T ASSUME ANYTHING AND DEAL DIRECTLY WITH THE OFFICE INTERNSHIP COORDINATOR TO BE SURE.

As Chief of Staff, I hired old interns all the time, or at the very least helped them find employment because they had proven themselves good people and good workers. If I didn't have a job for them, I certainly tried to help them out.

Getting an internship is not as easy as it used to be. Ten years ago, offices would generally take anyone for an internship position at anytime. Offices are stricter now, primarily because the Congressional handbooks say that interns "must perform services ...as part of a demonstrated educational plan." While this rule seems to put the kabash on any type of internship except for one associated with a college or university credit, it is not rigorously enforced and offices vary in their interpretation of it.

Moreover, as of May 2000, there are no forms that the office has to file indicating what "demonstrated educational plan" is associated with your internship. In fact, some House offices have their own internal forms which permit you to intern without being associated with any college or university.

However, it does help your chances if you can tell an office up front that you have prearranged to do the internship under the auspices a school or university. If you aren't enrolled anywhere, call an old college professor or someone else you know for advice. Pursue the internship whether or not you have made an arrangement — it's impossible to know an office's policy in advance. You'll eventually be apprised of their policy, and you can always let them know that you are in the process of securing an arrangement. I think a job on the Hill will be well worth the half-hour of phone calls it takes to set up an internship.

A popular, modified version of this approach is to intern for two or three days a week and find another job during the evenings or on your off days. This approach allows you to create a working relationship with the office ("Is John in today? I could really use him to...") while making enough money to pay rent. You will not gain as much experience as you would by being in the office five days a week, but you will still make substantial progress. D.C. has plenty of bars and restaurants that always need people, and it's easy to find work on evenings and weekends.

While interning in a Congressional office for free is the best way to get a job on the Hill, a big drawback to this approach is that it takes time and costs money. Most people can't easily afford to take off a month, move to Washington, and intern for free. This approach also requires you to commit yourself to getting a job on the Hill, pulling up stakes (at least temporarily) and heading to the shining city on a hill. I recommend giving it at least a two-month commitment — one month is too short in case it takes longer than you'd like to secure an internship or paid position. If you truly want to work on Capitol Hill, you're going to have to move to Washington eventually anyway, so you might as well just go for it.

So before we go to Step. 2, fully consider the internship route as a means to getting on Capitol Hill. Either internship route, full-time or part-time, requires you to move to Washington, D.C., and commit full-bore to getting a job on the Hill. While this may seem out of the question for many people, you're going to have a much, much more difficult — if not impossible — time pursuing the job from Paducah, Kentucky, or Modesto, California, or wherever you hang your hat. So think about it.

Inside Info: BECAUSE NOT EVERYONE CAN PICK UP AND MOVE TO WASHINGTON, PEOPLE OFTEN ASK ME WHETHER OR NOT AN INTERNSHIP IN A MEMBER'S DISTRICT OR HOME STATE OFFICE IS A GOOD TOOL TO GET A JOB ON CAPITOL HILL. MY ANSWER: IT'S THE BEST YOU CAN DO OUTSIDE OF WASHINGTON BUT THE LESS EFFECTIVE THAN ANY POSITION WHATSOEVER IN WASHINGTON. HALF THE BATTLE IS GETTING ON THE INSIDE OF CAPITOL HILL, AND A DISTRICT OR HOME STATE INTERNSHIP LIMITS YOUR CONTACTS TO ONE OFFICE. HOWEVER, FOR A TASTE OF POLITICAL LIFE, A DISTRICT OR HOME STATE OFFICE INTERNSHIP WILL GIVE YOU BETTER EXPERIENCE FOR YOUR RESUME THAN SOMEONE WHO HAS NEVER WORKED IN ANY CONGRESSIONAL ENVIRONMENT.

STEP 2. FIND SOMEONE ON THE INSIDE

Remember back on page 43, when I said that I helped people get jobs on the Hill even when I was an intern? I bet you said, "Yeah, right. A low-level intern schmuck couldn't really help someone get a job." I could and did, my friend, because I had a simple, unique advantage: access to the inside of Congress.

So the second step of The Plan is to find an insider to help you. Let's start by making two lists.

LIST #1 — SIX DEGREES OF WASHINGTON, D.C.

Take out a sheet of paper. List everyone you even vaguely know who works, or has worked, in Washington. Everyone's initial reaction to this list is "I don't know anyone who works in Washington." But take a moment to think about it. Pull out your address book. Go through a mental list of your friends and relatives, and your parents' friends and relatives, and your friends' friends and relatives. Usually, someone in your universe knows someone who works in Washington. I don't just mean people who have worked in Congress.

Think about government agencies, law firms, and associations. Someone who currently works, or has recently worked, in Congress, is ideal, but almost everyone in Washington has to deal with Congress at some point — so anyone associated with the federal government will definitely have contacts on the Hill.

If Kevin Bacon is only six degrees away, you can find someone who works, or has worked, in Washington. If you've gone through your Rolodex and found one person, you're in terrific shape. If you couldn't find anyone, that's OK, too. Don't fret. You'll definitely find someone on the next list to badger.

LIST #2 — WHERE I'VE HUNG MY HAT

Geography is an important thing to people on Capitol Hill. From a business point of view, Members of Congress have no reason to care about you unless you give them a reason to care. One of the best ways to get them to pay attention is to make a connection, however slight, to their district or state.

No matter where you are, you live in two Senators' home state and one Congressman/woman's district. Write down your zip code. Make a list of every place you've lived, every place you've gone to school, and every place you've worked. In general, just make a list of the places that you've been in your life for any amount of time. Even if you've spent your entire life in one place, it's one city and one state and that'll yield six contacts. I'll explain in a moment.

SO WHAT DO I DO WITH THESE LISTS?

Because so many people want jobs on Capitol Hill, the key is being in the right place at the right time — that is, being near someone who has the authority to hire when they want to hire. Timing is critical, and you have to do everything possible to get lucky.

Take a look at these two lists and the names on the list. What we're trying to do is find someone to be your connection to the inside of Congress and give you an informational interview. At the informational interview, you can find out if they know of any job openings and (if you've decided to do so) make your internship offer.

Many people loathe the informational interview; I'm usually one of them. The informational interview is much more effective in Congress than in the private sector because Capitol Hill is a community. It has its own restaurants, newspapers, and even its own vernacular. Unlike an informational interview with someone who only hears about jobs within their company, people on Capitol Hill hear about the job openings in all 535 individual companies (Representatives and Senators). In many ways, it's like trying to break into a small town where everyone knows each other (and the small town runs happens to run the government of the most powerful country on earth).

Take the first list, the Six Degrees of Washington people, and call them. If you have to, get their numbers from relatives, friends, or the internet. Call and introduce yourself. Remind them that you dated their brother or went to their Bar Mitzvah or their First Communion. Ask them if they know anyone in Congress who would be willing to talk with you about how to get a job on Capitol Hill.

Trust me, you're not the first and won't be the last person who has asked them for this type of help. Dealing with these requests is part of living and working in Washington. This is classic networking, only easier because people in D.C. are so used to these types of requests.

Now take the other list with the geographic locations. If you don't know the zip codes of these places already, go to the U.S. Postal Service's web page (http://www.usps.gov) and click on "zip codes." They have an extensive lookup feature that lets you put in a scant amount of information to deduce zip codes. After you get the relevant zip codes (err on the side of more, rather than less), log on http://www.YourCongress.com and use the Find Your Member feature to identify the exact Representatives and Senators who represent these areas. Some geographic areas (say,

San Francisco) will have more than one Member of Congress, but each zip code+4 within San Francisco has only one Representative and two Senators assigned to it. Also, use the profiles on YourCongress.com to get the phone numbers for their D.C. offices. Write them down.

On a Friday or Monday, call the Washington office of each Representative and Senator and ask to speak with his or her Chief of Staff. If the Chief of Staff takes your call — which is not likely, but possible on a Monday or Friday — introduce yourself, identify your connection to their district or state right away, tell them you're trying to get a job on Capitol Hill, and specifically ask if you can speak with them for an informational interview. You can arrange to talk on the phone, but it's better to do it in person.

Cold calling strangers is no fun. Whenever I needed people on my staff to make calls to Congressional offices to round up support for a bill, I always wrote them a script. Since you bought this book, I'll do the same for you. In the sample, just for fun, I've given you the worst name that ever existed: Joey Joe Joe Junior Shabado.

> *You: Hi, my name is Mr. Shabado, and I'm (a constituent or from the district or a friend of so and so). What's the name of your Chief of Staff?*

Answer: Lancelot Lockwood

You: Is (he or she) in?

You are likely to get sent to voicemail at this point. Live or voicemail, you have the same pitch.

You: Hi, Lancelot. My name is Joey Joe Joe Junior Shabado and I'm (a constituent or from the district or a friend of so and so). I am trying to get a job on the Hill and wanted to know if I could take a few minutes of your time for an informational interview [if you're asking for an informational interview over the phone, say so here] either now or at a more convenient time?

If you're speaking to them live, they'll probably make you repeat who you are and why you're calling. They're deciding whether or not to blow you off. Make sure to repeat your connection to their office.

If you're leaving a message on voicemail, make sure to leave a number at which they can call you back. If the area code is not in or near the Representative or Senator's district or home state, consider instead sending an email or calling back.

When you're done calling the Chiefs of Staff in each office, call back and repeat the whole scenario — only this time you should ask for the Legislative Director.

After your first call, wait a week and then call again. Don't be put off when people don't return your call. As my first boss told me, "Your calls were noted but not returned." When he had a position to talk about, he took the call. In a way, it's your first true Congressional test: can you persist long enough to make someone give a damn about you?

Which leads us to...

STEP 3. DON'T GIVE UP

I once overheard Jim McDermott, who is currently a Congressman from Washington State, upon receiving good news over the telephone say, "By God, this business isn't for the pretty or the strong, it's for the persistent." This statement is true about so many facets of life in Congress, and definitely applies to getting your first job on the Hill.

Consider my own situation. During college, I interned twice a week for an office for a year. After I graduated, I assumed that I would get a job in that office. Yet, because the office had unusually low turnover, no positions in that office had opened up. So I waited, took a job in the government affairs department of a trade association, and kept searching for a position on the Hill. I left a consistent but not overbearing string of voicemails (matter of fact, no sign of panic) on the Hill to my old contacts. A few months later, a position opened up. I interviewed for the position, and I got the job.

Inside Info: EXPECT THAT MOST CHIEFS OF STAFF OR LEGISLATIVE DIRECTORS WILL NOT TAKE YOUR CALL ON THE FIRST TRY. TO INCREASE YOUR CHANCE OF GETTING THROUGH TO THEM, TRY CALLING ON A FRIDAY AFTERNOON OR MONDAY MORNING. BECAUSE CONGRESS IS ALMOST NEVER IN SESSION AT THESE TIMES, OFFICES ARE MORE RELAXED AND LIKELY TO TAKE YOUR CALL.

Odds are that you won't have to pursue a job as long as I did, but you should be prepared for anything. Congress has many tests of persistence, and getting a job is almost certain to be your first one. The simple fact is that too many people want these jobs relative to how many jobs there are. You have to be prepared to dig in for the long haul.

V.
You've Got An Interview - Woo Hoo!

If you follow The Plan, eventually the stars will align and you'll be granted an interview. Congratulations! This is your big chance. Whether it's for a paid position or simply an informational interview, it's a great opportunity.

I. INTERVIEW PREPARATION

One of the most pivotal things you can do in your quest to get a job on Capitol Hill is take a shower and comb your hair. Nobody, except maybe Members with large numbers of environmentalist supporters, likes smelly employees. After hygiene, the next important thing to do is research the Member of Congress with whom you are interviewing. Research will help you get a sense of his or her reputation and their professional

IF YOU HAVE ANY PARTY AFFILIATION ON YOUR RESUME, IT IS POINTLESS TO INTERVIEW FOR A PAID POSITION WITH A MEMBER FROM ANOTHER PARTY.* DON'T ASSUME THAT THIS DISMISSAL IS ANOTHER FUNCTION OF WASHINGTON INFIGHTING AND CONSPIRACIES — IT'S NOT. RATHER, IT IS A BASIC WEEDING-OUT FUNCTION. WHEN YOU HAVE 200 RESUMES FOR A $20,000 A YEAR JOB, THE QUICKEST WAY TO WEED DOWN THE STACK IS TO TOSS OUT ANYONE FROM THE OTHER PARTY. IN ALMOST ALL CIRCUMSTANCES, 99.9% OF THE TIME, YOU'D RATHER GIVE THE JOB TO SOMEONE IN YOUR OWN PARTY, SO WHY GO THROUGH THE HASSLE OF TALKING TO SOMEONE YOU WON'T WANT TO HIRE ANYWAY?

*The only exception to this rule is an internship. You can get away with being in the other party for an internship in school, although even that might even raise a small flag. Be prepared to talk about it.

political interests.

Your first piece of homework is to log on www.YourCongress.com and look up the profiles of the Representative or Senator. Notice that you'll also find links to the their official home pages — we'll get to that later. The profiles will give you an overview of their background, personal information, and committee assignments.

Next, I suggest reading the profiles of the Member and their district or state in two publications: *Politics in America,* published by Congressional Quarterly, and the *Almanac of American Politics,* published by the National

Journal. Both of these are thick, heavy reference volumes that can be found at your local library or can be purchased at most bookstores or through the web. These profiles will give you more in-depth information on their reputation, their legislative initiatives, and the interests of their district or state.

Inside Info: WHAT ABOUT THE INTERN COORDINATOR? MANY OFFICES HAVE AN INTERN COORDINATOR, AND I ASSURE YOU THAT EVERY ONE OF THEM LISTENS TO THE CHIEF OF STAFF OR LEGISLATIVE DIRECTOR. IF YOU TRY TO SECURE AN INTERNSHIP THROUGH THE INTERN COORDINATOR, YOU LOSE THE CHANCE TO GET ASSISTANCE FROM THE CHIEF OF STAFF OR LEGISLATIVE DIRECTOR. DON'T WASTE YOUR TIME WITH INTERN COORDINATORS UNLESS YOU'RE DIRECTED TO BY THE CHIEF OF STAFF OR LD.

Then, use the link through the profile page on www.YourCongress.com and go to the Member's official web page. Look for where the Representative or Senator posts their recent press releases; pull up the last couple months' worth and pay special attention to them. These are the best indicators of the Member's interests and values.

Put more stock in a Member's press releases than anything written by reporters. While the reporters who write the *Politics in America* and *Almanac of American Politics* books are usually very good, often times the Representative or Senator might not think so. There's a chance that they take exception to the characterizations contained in the Congressional Quarterly or National Journal book. If they wrote that Congresswoman So and So is a tried and true liberal, and the Congresswoman has been working hard to dispel this image, the office won't be too happy if you talk about how you want to work for her because she's left of the Communist Party.

After you look at their press releases, read their bio to get a general sense of what they say they're all about. Relying on the web page information best prepares you for an interview because it is closer to the source — the Representative or Senator.

II. INFORMATIONAL INTERVIEW TIPS

If you've got your interview for a paid position all lined up, you might want to skip this section (but I bet you might learn something if you stick around).

Your job in the informational interview is to:

a. Show the interviewer that you are not a wacko

b. Find out if they know of any job openings (in their office or otherwise)

c. Ask for their advice on your Hill search

d. Ask them for additional contacts, and

e. If you've decided to go this route, offer your services as an intern.

The keys in the informational interview are to be polite and brief. You've asked someone for his or her time, not the other way around. Don't wear out your welcome.

Before you go to the interview, practice delivering a quick, 10-second synopsis of your personal experience and your goal (entry-level staff assistant/LC/LA position). I recommend that you practice this 10-second personal experience/goal segment out loud so you can say it in your sleep. Being able to clearly convey who you are and why you're there will help gain their confidence very quickly.

When you arrive, have your resume and cover letter ready to hand them. Thank them for taking the time to meet with you. Deliver your 10-second synopsis, and segue right into asking him or her if they know of any open positions. Have a pen and paper ready to write down any information they provide. Ask them for their advice on the best way to get a job on Capitol Hill.

CAUTION: WHATEVER YOU DO, DON'T ASK TO BE PAID FOR YOUR INTERNSHIP BECAUSE IT WILL CUT YOUR CHANCE OF GETTING THE POSITION TO ZERO. YOU WILL LOOK NAÏVE. COULD AN OFFICE PAY YOU? SURE. WILL THEY? HECK, NO. HIRING AN INTERN MEANS MORE PAPERWORK AND HASSLE. MORE IMPORTANTLY, VERY FEW OFFICES PAY THEIR INTERNS ANYTHING FOR ONE REASON – WHY BUY THE COW WHEN YOU CAN HAVE THE MILK FOR FREE?

When you ask for their advice on how to get a job on Capitol Hill, you have an opportunity to listen to their wisdom — make sure to be interested and engaged. After you've established rapport, let them know that you're willing to work as an intern.

As a closing topic of conversation, ask them if they know of anyone else that you could talk to on an informational basis. If they like you, and they have some friends, they'll likely give you some names. If they don't like you, they might send you to some of their enemies. Either way, you're making more connections.

Don't force conversation. If you've gone through the items and you've gotten any additional information (names or otherwise), politely thank them for their time and skedaddle. Send a thank you note or email within a week or so.

Then do it all over again with the next person on the list. Lather. Rinse. Repeat.

III. THREE THINGS AND TWO QUESTIONS FOR AN INTERVIEW WITH A CHIEF OF STAFF

If you've gotten the call for an interview for a paid position with a Congressional office, congratulations! You're part of a select group. You're now in the final stages of competing for a very unique job.

It is likely that your only interview will be with the Chief of Staff. Some offices have you interview with the Chief of Staff and then the Member of Congress, but for an entry-level position it's quite possible you'll never meet the Big Guy or Big Gal until after you've been hired. Some offices also make you spend time with everyone on staff before getting hired to pass the Team Chemistry test. Each office is different, so you should find out their "process" when you are called to schedule an interview.

MORE HOMEWORK

I know you thought those darn lists wouldn't come in handy again, but they will. Blow the dust off them, and call the people in Washington with whom you have developed even a modicum of a relationship. Even if they are only people who gave you an informational interview, call them on a Friday or Monday and ask for their opinion of the Representative or Senator's office where you are interviewing. People in D.C. love to talk about other Members of Congress and their staffs, so they'll be happy to give you a sense of the other office's reputation. Another good possibility is that they know someone in that office and can put in a call to help you.

Any feedback you get is good. Don't be alarmed if someone warns you against working for a particular Member. Don't cancel the interview, either, based on someone else's assessment. Just make note of their opinion — don't let it bother you right now.

In addition to all the things that you should do for the informational interview, there are Three Things You Should Plan to Talk About during your interview with the Chief of Staff.

FIRST THING TO TALK ABOUT: HAVE ONE MAIN ISSUE OF INTEREST

In the course of the interview, regardless of the postion, it's likely that you will be asked exactly what issues you are interested in. If you're anything like I was at the time, you would be willing to cover basket weaving as an issue if they would just give you the job. While this may be the case, there is a still a core idealism that persists within all Hill staffers, even jaded old veteran ones (like the one who will probably interview you), which wants to hear that you care about something. Everybody needs a shtick.

So before your interview, think about the issues that you do really care about. Go back to the issue list on page 14 and look through it again. Has your life been affected by any particular issue? Do certain issues intrigue you? Were you involved in something as a kid? As a young kid, gun violence was something that affected my life, so during my interviews I said this was an issue that concerned me greatly. Think about what you care about, and make certain to be able to mention at least one issue. The Chief of Staff won't expect you to know the issue in depth, so don't spend hours at the library trying to be proficient at it. Even if you know a lot about it, you have no idea how it plays on the Hill. Use the opportunity to demonstrate that you are an involved person, but don't get on your soapbox. You don't want to accidentally turn your interviewer off by sounding cocky.

SECOND THING TO TALK ABOUT: HOW THE MEMBER WINS.

I vividly remember interviewing a person for a press position who said, "I say my piece, and I fight for what I think is right, but in the end the Member wins. I do what they say." This was one of the best statements I had ever heard in an interview. It showed a keen understanding of a staffer's role: do your job full bore, but, in the end, the Representative or Senator makes the call. This maxim applies to every position in a Congressional office.

It might sound a little ironic, but the last person anyone on Capitol Hill wants to hire is someone with an agenda. Avoid, at all costs, being an "Intense Agenda Person." If you are someone with a cause, I urge you to check it at the door. The only people who survive working in politics professionally are those who can sustain an even keel. People who care about something so deeply that they would, for example, blow up a federal building, are the same type of people that will put the cause over the interests of the person who is paying their salary. Talking about how, in the end, "the Member wins" will dispel any concern the interviewer might have.

Inside Info: THERE ARE THREE QUESTIONS, BY LAW, THAT CONGRESSIONAL OFFICES ARE ALLOWED TO ASK PROSPECTIVE EMPLOYEES IN AN INTERVIEW THAT ARE NOT PERMITTED IN THE PRIVATE SECTOR: RESIDENCY, POLITICAL VIEWS, AND TO WHOM YOU'RE RELATED. CONGRESSIONAL OFFICES CAN DISCRIMINATE BASED ON WHERE YOU LIVE AND WHAT YOUR POLITICS ARE. MOREOVER, ANTI-NEPOTISM LAWS PROHIBIT THEM FROM HIRING YOU IF YOU'RE RELATED TO THE REPRESENTATIVE OR SENATOR.

MOST OF THE QUESTIONS A CHIEF OF STAFF WILL ASK ARE DESIGNED TO GET A PEEK INTO HOW YOU WILL BE AS A PERSON ON A STAFF. CONGRESSIONAL OFFICES, PARTICULARLY ON THE HOUSE SIDE, ARE ORGANIZATIONS IN CLOSE QUARTERS, SO THE CHIEF OF STAFF IS LOOKING FOR YOUR FIT WITHIN THE OFFICE. THE BEST ADVICE I CAN GIVE TO YOU IS TO BE YOURSELF. (I KNOW. LAME, BUT TRUE, ADVICE.) CHIEFS OF STAFF CAN SMELL A FAKE A MILE AWAY, SO ANY ATTEMPT TO CAREFULLY CHOOSE YOUR WORDS WILL COST YOU SOME POINTS.

THIRD THING TO TALK ABOUT: WILLINGNESS TO DO WHAT IT TAKES

A Chief of Staff is in charge of a team and the last thing they want to deal with is staff bickering and infighting. Ultimately, what every Chief of Staff wants is someone who takes initiative to get their job done and is also willing to do any other job that might come up. Often times, particularly during election season, Congressional offices undertake tasks that require immense amounts of staff resources — getting out mailings, making phone calls, or traveling to the district. Often, the entire Congressional staff is required to pitch in. This means that staff can't be concerned with titles and should only be concerned about getting the job done.

By conveying to the interviewer your willingness "to do what it takes," you will convey two important things: the right priorities and an understanding of what goes on in a Congressional office. I guarantee this tip will score you points and separate you from the competition.

WHY QUESTIONS ARE YOUR FRIENDS

At the end of your interview with the Chief of Staff (and also the Representative or Senator, if they interview you as well), you will definitely be given a chance to ask questions.

Questions are a pivotal part of the interview — it's the one time you can control what is discussed. It's your last chance to separate yourself from the rest of the candidates. As someone who interviewed lots of potential job candidates who decided to stay quiet, at this point, it's definitely to your advantage to ask questions. In fact, asking the rights ones can make all the difference in the world.

QUESTIONS FOR THE CHIEF OF STAFF

Every person a Chief of Staff hires reflects upon them. They want you to do the job for which you're hired, but they're also concerned about the staff functioning well as a whole and long-term staff development. Over the years, a few questions I have been asked during interviews have stood out to me. When you're given the golden opportunity of asking questions, you can't lose with these two.

1. How would you describe the Member's relationship with his staff?

There are two things you are trying to discover with this question: one is office policy toward access to the Member, and the other is his or her temperament. Some Members have a very close relationship with their staff and try to establish a collaborative setting. Other Members keep a distance between their staff and themselves.

The response you get to this question will be a good indicator of how much access you, as a staff member, will get to the Member. The better the access, the better the chance of establishing a close relationship. The closer the relationship, the better chance you'll be able to earn his or her trust and get things done. It's also quite likely that the closer the relationship you have, the more you'll enjoy your job.

Getting a sense of your boss' temperament will help you evaluate whether or not you want to work in that office, or at the very least warn you about the pitfalls of your potential working environment. Some Members are yellers. Other Members are passive-aggressive and brood. Regardless of your boss' temperament, you can count on encountering very stressful times in the Capitol Hill environment. Behavior that's tough to deal with is part of the business because there are times when it seems that so much is at stake. It's useful to know, up front, how your potential boss deals with these situations.

Obviously, few offices will outright admit that their boss is a complete wacko so it requires some reading between the lines. If you do your homework, you should know before you walk into the interview if the office has a history of staff problems or the Representative or Senator is known to be a serious nut-job.

2. How is the entire organization structured, and what is your relationship with your district or home state office (or offices)?

This question will give you insight into who's really in charge of the operation, as well as a sense of the office's overall workplace health. Furthermore, it will demonstrate a high-level understanding of Capitol Hill.

Almost all Capitol Hill offices experience at least mild tension with their district offices. A Member's Washington office tends to do policy work, district offices tend to do constituent services (casework), and the different responsibilities mean different constituencies. In the midst of these competing interests, district offices often feel unappreciated. (Frankly, a Representative or Senator can get away with a mediocre Washington office but decent constituent service from the district office is a necessity.) If there is no established mechanism for dealing with these tensions, they can affect the entire staff.

In addition, personality conflicts between a district director and a Chief of Staff can exacerbate any inter-office problem. Most often, the organizational structure answers questions about who's in charge, but in some offices structures are less well defined. If tensions exist because of a lack of leadership, or internal strife, it's good to get a sense of these problems before you go into the office.

If you feel like there is tension between the offices or between people, it isn't a topic that should be pursued. Just make a mental note and move on.

IV: TIPS FOR INTERVIEWING WITH THE REPRESENTATIVE OR SENATOR: TWO QUESTIONS TO ASK AND ONE CARD TO PLAY

If you do interview with a Representative or Senator, know that they require a different approach than the Chief of Staff. Since Members operate on a different level than the Chief of

Staff, they will have their own perspective. It's virtually impossible to know what an individual Representative or Senator is looking for in an interview. If you feel that your interview with the Chief of Staff went well, you might consider asking him or her for advice in preparing for the meeting with the Representative or Senator. If they were impressed with you, they may give you inside tips.

These are three items that you can always use in an interview with any Representative or Senator:

1. Ask: "What is the Most Important Quality You Expect in Your Staff?"

In their first response to this question, a Representative or Senator will likely spew their latest beef with someone on their staff. If, earlier that day, the Representative or Senator didn't get a memo on time, he or she will say they want things on time. If somebody missed an important event, they'll say they expect staff to "stay on top of things."

Listen to their initial response, but ignore it. Wait for their second one, and take it to heart. Their second response will be the more important one. If it has not yet been discussed, let the Member of Congress know that you believe in loyalty. Every elected official wants loyal staff. Think of this question as providing a chance for you to give the "In the end, the Member wins" speech to the Member.

2. Ask: "Why Did You Run for Congress?"

This is a great question to ask because it gives the Representative or Senator a chance to talk about their purpose for being in Congress. All Representatives and Senators have told this story a thousand times, and if they have been in Congress for a long time, it has changed a thousand times. Nonetheless, this question should provide insight into his or her basic motivation for running for Congress, as well as a personal sketch of their current view of the job.

During the interview, this question will give you a moment to let someone else do the talking. There's no angle to this question, so don't read too much into it. I have given this question as advice to countless people, and can honestly say that it has always yielded productive answers which helped them decide whether or not to work for a particular Congressman/woman or Senator.

3. Play the Local Card

If you have lived or worked in the district or state the Representative or Senator represents, currently or previously, make sure to mention it. All Members of Congress believe that hiring someone from their own district or state is a professional and political plus. In all facets of Congressional work, a staff member that has a sense of the geography, culture, and values of a region and its people is always one step ahead of someone who has to learn these things. In addition to likely being better employees, it is politically advantageous for a Representative or Senator to hire local folks. If he or she hires someone from the district, they know that your friends and relatives will now associate you with them — that's an immediate local political reward.

Don't worry if you don't currently live in their district or state. Any connection you can make, regardless of the time frame, will put you ahead of someone with no local relevance. Remember, your local connection shows a familiarity with the geography, culture, and their constituents. When you gained that familiarity is not that important.

In 1990, after three or four interviews for various positions on Capitol Hill, I had my first interview with an actual Member of Congress - and it was with my hometown Congresswoman. I was one of two people competing for a legislative correspondent job. I didn't have any idea what to expect, and I really didn't

IF YOU WANT TO KNOW HOW MUCH AN OFFICE PAYS A CERTAIN POSITION, THERE IS A WAY TO GET A GOOD IDEA. EVERY QUARTER, THE HOUSE AND SENATE CLERKS PUBLISH BOOKS (CALLED THE STATEMENT OF DISBURSEMENTS AND THE "GREEN BOOK," RESPECTIVELY) THAT LIST THE NAME OF EACH CONGRESSIONAL STAFFER AND THE AMOUNT THEY WERE PAID FOR THE LAST QUARTER. IF YOU FEEL COMFORTABLE, CALL ONE OF YOUR CONTACTS ON CAPITOL HILL AND ASK HIM OR HER TO LOOK UP WHAT AN OFFICE HAS PREVIOUSLY PAID PEOPLE IN THE SAME POSITION (SALARIES ARE PUBLISHED IN QUARTER-YEARS, SO YOU HAVE TO MULTIPLY BY FOUR). WHILE YOU WON'T SPECIFICALLY KNOW WHY THEY PAID THAT PERSON THAT AMOUNT, THE FIGURES WILL GIVE YOU A GENERAL IDEA OF SALARY RANGES. AND YOU CAN SEE HOW MUCH THE CHIEF OF STAFF WHO IS INTERVIEWING YOU MAKES!

know what I was doing, but I did have one ace-in-the-hole: the local card. During the interview, we started talking about places we both knew, which led to people we both knew. I started to feel very comfortable, and before I knew it, I had the job.

After I was hired, my boss told me who didn't get the job: Eleanor Mondale, the daughter of former Vice-President, who had the political name but not the hometwon connection. (Eleanor went on to become a well-known journalist, so I think she's probably gotten past it.) The power of the local card can trump almost anything, so if you've got it, play it.

FOLLOW-UP

After the interview, make certain to follow-up with the office. Some offices take longer to hire than others, so don't be put off if you don't hear back from them immediately. Call the Chief of Staff to check in and see where he or she is in the hiring decision. Remember that Congressional offices are so busy that they may have had every intention of hiring you, but were distracted by the press of regular business. When I interviewed for my second job on Capitol Hill, three months went by between the interview with the Member and the offer — and my old boss swears on her grave that it was just because they were so damn busy.

THE OFFER

There has been a big shift over time in the strategies that people who are new to the job market employ in dealing with salary offers. When I got my first job on the Hill, I was so glad to have a job offer — any offer — that I didn't even dare to think about arguing over money. The job market was different then, however, and unemployment was much higher. The workplace has changed dramatically in the last ten years, and during my last round of hiring (in 1999) more than half of the new hires wanted to dicker over salary.

My best advice is not to dicker over money, particularly for an entry-level position. While the Chief of Staff and the Representative or Senator may think you're great, they're not going to overpay for the position. If you feel that you must counter-offer, go ahead, but you're likely to find yourself on the uncomfortable receiving end of a "Sorry, take it or leave it" proposition, in which case you may be bitter. If you must counteroffer, ask for a review in six months — this is something they're likely to give you in lieu of upfront cash. Once you prove yourself, you'll be in good position to leverage more cash out of your boss.

AN OFFER FROM A WACKO

Since I don't recommend canceling an interview just because you get some negative feedback during the research process, you might be offered a position from the office of a Representative or Senator that has a reputation for being a wacko. There's a saying in Washington: "Every rumor you hear is true." Therefore, odds are that the reputation is well deserved.

That said, the bottom line is that unless you have another offer in hand, or are real close, take the job. Your job is to get on the inside of Congress. Once inside Congress, you can always look for another job. Be prepared for things to be a little tough, gain some experience, and ride the position to the next opportunity.

VI.
Alternative Paths: Other Options on and Around Capitol Hill

This book may have raised some doubts for you about working for a Member of Congress. Or you might not be able to secure a job on Capitol Hill right away. In either case, there are a number of jobs options in Washington.

However, if you are interested in using an off-Capitol Hill position as a bridge to getting a job with a House or Senate Member, you should set your goals for pre-Hill employment. Your goals with any non-Hill job should be two-fold:

1. Keep in contact with the Hill to learn about open positions.
2. Gain experience that makes you more employable on the Hill.

Applicable work experience includes following issues on Capitol Hill, writing issue memos on almost anything, attending hearings or markups, representing your organization at political events, and going on lobbying visits.

These are some other options that you can explore if you find that getting your dream job is taking much longer than you anticipated.

CAPITOL HILL JOBS NOT IN A REPRESENTATIVE OR SENATOR'S OFFICE

Working in the Congressional office of a Representative or Senator has been the focus of this book, but Capitol Hill also has other offices which have jobs which help run the business of Congress (remember those non-partisan jobs in mentioned near the beginning of the book?): Office of the Clerk, Office of the Sergeant at Arms, Chief Administrative Officer, House Information Resources, Superintendent's Office, Procurement Office, Office of Legislative Counsel, Office of the Inspector General, Media Services, Architect of the Capitol, Senate Office Operations, Secretary of the Senate, Capitol Police, and many others. To see a sampling of additional offices on Capitol Hill that may have positions, log on http://www.house.gov/Party _organizations.html or http://www.aoc.gov, or http://www.house.gov/house/govsites.

WORKING IN A DEPARTMENT OR AGENCY

Working in an executive branch agency (Department of Agriculture, Treasury, etc., or an office under their direction) is a path that I would least recommend for two main reasons. First, government agency jobs tend to have lengthy and laborious hiring processes. Lengthy forms, waiting periods, multiple interviews, and excessive government blah-blah can wear you out before an actual hiring decision is made. Secondly, and more importantly, I don't know anyone who likes to get things done who is happy at an executive branch agency.

Inside any executive branch agency, there are two classes of workers: political appointments and career appointments. Career people generally stick around regardless of who the President (and their relevant Secretary) is. They are the institutional knowledge in the organization and really know how to make things happen or, in most cases, not make things happen. On the other hand, political appointees in the agencies are handpicked by the current Presidential Administration, and often want to get things done. Unfortunately, they usually lack the ability to move the entrenched bureaucracy.

If you want to become one of the unaccountable thousands whose sole objective is to collect a check, agency jobs are for you. I have a feeling, however, since you bought this book that you don't fall into this class.

WORKING IN A TRADE ASSOCIATION OR LAW FIRM

Washington is full of associations. Some of them you've heard of: the American Medical Association, the National Rifle Association, the National Education Association. Some of them you probably haven't heard of: the Snack Food Association, the American Association of Otolaryngology, and the Yellow Pages Publishers Association.

Part of all these associations' missions is to keep an eye on what is going on in Washington, and usually Congress is one of their biggest targets (agency regulations are the other big ticket). Working for an association — almost any association — allows you to stay in touch with, and learn about, the rhythms of Congress. As a result, associations are usually good places in which to enhance your resume while waiting for a position to open up on the Hill.

WORKING IN A NON-PROFIT

Non-profits are similar to trade associations and have the same goals with respect to Congress. However, they carry greater risks in terms of employment. Anybody who has spent anytime around different types of organizations knows that people in non-profits are usually well meaning but tend to be disorganized. In a non-profit, you are more likely to find an issue that you care about and "feel good" about your job, but you are less likely to gain work experience applicable to Congress.

While this view of non-profits sounds negative, it pays to evaluate each situation based on the people you meet. If the office is small and you will have direct contact with one of the non-profit's top people, it could be a good situation. As a building block for your career, the right situation could give you the chance to shine by taking the initiative and shaping up a foundering organization.

CONGRESSIONAL EMPLOYEES ARE PROHIBITED FROM DOING CAMPAIGN WORK. AS A RESULT, A FEW MONTHS BEFORE AN ELECTION, SOME CONGRESSIONAL OFFICES MOVE A COUPLE OF THEIR EMPLOYEES TO THEIR CAMPAIGN OFFICES. AS A RESULT, YOU CAN OFTEN GET A TEMPORARY PAID POSITION IN A CONGRESSIONAL OFFICE TO HELP OUT WHILE THEIR REGULAR STAFF IS ON HIATUS. IT'S A GOOD OPPORTUNITY TO GET INSIDE CONGRESS, AND GET PAID, ON A SHORT-TERM BASIS.

WORKING IN THE CAMPAIGN WORLD

Campaigns are big business. Members of Congress

and Senators spend millions of dollars on fundraising, direct mail, polling, media consultants, field consultants, and other campaign personnel. As a result, there are hundreds of companies in Washington that conduct business in all these areas. They tend to be small firms that likely need administrative support. Working in one of these offices will give you contact with their clients on Capitol Hill, and is a good way to meet a select group of people on the inside of Congress.

There are also the national party committees: the Democratic Congressional Campaign Committee, the National Republican Congressional Committee, the Republican Senatorial Campaign Committee, and the Democratic Senatorial Campaign Committee. These are large national organizations which deal solely with campaigning and fundraising, and are perpetually in need of people. While none of these organizations are known to be great places to work, you can earn a party loyalty stripe and use any of them as a stepping-stone to Capitol Hill.

WORKING FOR A GAMER

Washington is a town that plays games. Persuasion is a game, and providing the means of getting the information across is a game, too. Washington relies on printed material, information systems, and entertainment as means to its many-headed ends. Many industries thrive in and around Congress by helping people get messages into the Capitol, by producing printed or other promotional materials to send to Members or to the membership of various organizations, or catering events that feature Members. You will have little to no problem finding work with any of these industries while you try and get a job on the Hill.

WORKING IN A BAR OR RESTAURANT

D.C. has no shortage of bars or restaurants that are always willing to hire people on a short-term basis. I know a number of recent college grads who work four days a week at a bar or restaurant and intern for two days a week on the Hill.

LINE SITTING

Believe it or not, line sitting — holding a place in line — is an actual job in Washington. There are listings in the phone book for line sitting services. The committees that have high-profile hearings or markups (read: ones with lots of cash at stake) often generate enormous lines waiting to get into the hearing room. Lobbyists actually pay people to wait in line for them, sometimes days in advance. When the hour of the hearing gets close enough, the lobbyist simply exchange places with their line sitter. Often, a line sitter stands (no sitting allowed) for eight or nine hours.

VII.
Conclusion

While I may sound a little cynical, I still love Congress. It is an institution without parallel. There is no place on this planet where the confluence of people and ideas comes together like Capitol Hill. Personally, working on Capitol Hill teaches you a tremendous amount about your own values and beliefs, as well as your strengths and weaknesses.

As an American, working on Capitol Hill gives you a view of our country that very few people get to see. It is a view that celebrates our diversity, unearths our fissures, but ultimately reaffirms our common principles.

Most Members of Congress are extraordinarily good people doing a very difficult and thankless job. They give up their lives and risk their families to serve their country. Being part of their world for any amount of time is a unique, illuminating experience.

I guarantee you won't regret working on Capitol Hill. In the meantime, if there is anything I can ever do to help, don't hesitate to contact me at chris@yourcongress.com. After you've been on the Hill for a while, and have a good tale to tell, feel free to send your Capitol Hill stories to myhillstory@yourcongress.com. We might even send you something.

VIII.
Appendix of Resources

USEFUL WEBSITES

www.house.gov/cao-hr/employme.htm

The Chief Administrative Officer of the House lists vacancy announcements every Monday at this web address. It is, by no means, an exhaustive list, but it's a starting point.

www.asaenet.org/careers

The American Society of Association Executives has an online "career center" where metro D.C. trade association and non-profits post job openings. They have a free online searchable database, and you can sort based on salary, type of position, level of position, and region of the country.

www.workincongress.com

This is YourCongress.com's site for people looking to find a job on Capitol Hill. It is designed to have useful information, tips, and helpful updates for Congress job seekers.

data.georgetown.edu/student-affiars/och

This site is Georgetown University's guide to D.C. neighborhoods, and is very useful if you're about to get in the truck and move to Washington, D.C. It also includes information on the Virginia and Maryland suburbs.

www.washingtoncitypaper.com/class/housing_for_rent.html

This is Washington's City Paper's listing of housing for rent in the Washington, D.C. area. It is one of the most extnesive lists available on the web, but there is a trick to it. Even though the paper doesn't come out until Thursday, the website and rental section is updated on Tuesday, and many listings are gone by Thursday.

www.RollCall.com

Roll Call is one of two Capitol Hill newspapers, and it's terrific. They have an online version which is useful, although not as in-depth as the paper version. Roll Call gives quality, in-depth coverage of "inside baseball," and it's read by everyone on Capitol Hill. You'll often see classified advertisements for positions in Congressional offices, too. It's published twice a week.

www.HillNews.com

The Hill is a newer Capitol Hill newspaper which has improved dramatically over the last couple years. It currently comes out once a week.

www.WashingtonPost.com

The Washington Post's website is an amazingly useful website for all things related to life in Washington. It has the latest developments on Capitol Hill, lists of current happenings, real estate listings, community information, and all kinds of useful tools.

www.c-f-m.org

The Congressional Management Foundation is an organization which exisits to help the offices of Representatives and Senators improve their mangement practices. This site has salary data for House and Senate positions, and lots of other useful reports. Some information is provided on the site, some you might have to order through CMF.

House of Representatives Job Line: 202-225-2450, then press 7

The House Office of Human Resources provides this service, and the vacancy announcements are updated weekly. A Chief of Staff calls this office when they have a position available. The Office of Human Resources then assigns a vacancy number, posts a blind listing, collects resumes that respond to the announcement, and then forwards the resumes to the Chief of Staff. Responding to an individual listing is a good way to get your resume in front of a Chief of Staff.

After calling this number, pressing 7 gets you to the vacancy announcements. Follow the instructions. You'll likely want to press 2 for Member and Committee positions (3 is for computer and technical positions and 4 is for other administrative positions). The information is updated every week. The recording will indicate only the vacancy number and the title of the open position. The main shortcoming of the House Job Line is that it doesn't tell you which Representative has the open position, nor his or her party affiliation.

All vacancy numbers start with MEM, and are followed by two series of numbers — write them down, they're important. A frequently overlooked feature of this job line is that you can respond to a specific vacancy announcement by fax (202-226-0098).

The House Job Line also has an option to send your resume to a general box at the Resume Referral Office. I have never heard of anyone actually getting a job through this service, and I don't recommend it.

Senate Job Line: 202-228-JOBS

Much like the House line, simply call the number and follow the instructions. The Senate Job Line is very similar to the House's, only better. Their listings include the entire job description submitted by the office. As a result of having more information, you'll know with much more certainty whether or not the open position is right for you. The Senate Job Line also has a separate category for press positions.

IN PERSON

Senate Placement Office (202-224-9167)

The Senate Placement Office is open from 830AM-530PM Monday to Friday. The Senate publishes a Weekly Employment Bulletin that is available in their office every Tuesday. They are located in Room 142 of the Hart Building, a little over a block from the Capitol.

If you want to be considered for jobs that are not advertised publicly, the Senate Placement Office offers a unique service. Anyone can walk in, wait, and get an informational interview on any business day between the hours of 10AM–12PM, and 1PM-3PM (except Friday, when they knock off an hour earlier). Make sure to have your resume and other materials when you arrive.

House Office of Human Resources (202-225-2450)

You can walk into the House Human Resources Office from 9AM–6PM, Monday to Friday, and look through new job listings published every Monday. They are located in Room 263 of the Cannon Building, across the street from the Capitol. Unlike the Senate, they don't give informational interviews.

ABOUT YOURCONGRESS.COM

YourCongress.com was founded in 1999 to provide an easy and entertaining way to find out what's going on in Congress.

For more information about YourCongress.com, log on http://www.YourCongress.com, toll-free phone or fax to 877-240-9097, or drop us a line at YourCongress.com, P.O. Box 1661, Arlington, VA, 22210.

ABOUT THE AUTHOR

Christopher Porter is the Founder and CEO of YourCongress.com. In 1985, Christopher interned for Congresswoman Mary Rose Oakar (Cleveland, Ohio) and later joined her staff full-time in 1990. He served as Legislative Director for Congresswoman Elizabeth Furse (Portland, Oregon) and Co-Policy Director of the Congressional Diabetes Caucus from 1993 until 1998.

After Congresswoman Furse retired in 1998, Porter worked as Chief of Staff to Congressman David Wu. He left in late 1999 to launch YourCongress.com. Thanks to his appearance on *Who Wants to Be a Millionaire,* he is painfully aware that Will Rogers, not Mae West, said, "I never met a man I didn't like." He and his wife Rosalyn, and their son Stephen, live in Arlington, Virginia.

Christopher can be reached at chris@YourCongress.com.

ACKNOWLEDGEMENTS

Rosalyn Porter, for her constant love and support; Loretta, Elizabeth, and Mary Rose, the other important women in my life; Tom Porter, for advice and life-line support; Jenny Eshelman Hunter, for editing skills; Tom Albert, my mentor; Joel Wood, for being the first to say "hire this man" and being a friend ever since; and David Wu, for just being David.